BUNTING'S

Moya Cannon is an Irish poet with six previous collections. In 2021 Carcanet published her *Collected Poems*. She was born and grew up in Co. Donegal, received a BA in History and Politics from University College, Dublin, and an MPhil in International Relations from Corpus Christi College, Cambridge. A recipient of the inaugural Brendan Behan Award and of the O'Shaughnessy Award, she was Heimbold Professor of Irish Studies at Villanova University and in 2004 was elected to Áosdána, the affiliation of Irish creative artists.

BUNTING'S HONEY
MOYA CANNON

CARCANET POETRY

First published in Great Britain in 2025 by
Carcanet
Main Library, The University of Manchester
Oxford Road, Manchester, M13 9PP
www.carcanet.co.uk

A CIP catalogue record for this book is
available from the British Library.

ISBN 978 1 80017 489 4

Book design by Andrew Latimer, Carcanet
Typesetting by LiteBook Prepress Services
Printed in Great Britain by SRP Ltd, Exeter, Devon

The publisher acknowledges financial
assistance from Arts Council England.

Contents

for Brendan and Ursula Flynn

'we are continually overflowing toward those who preceded us, toward our origin, and toward those who seemingly come after us… It is our task to imprint this temporary, perishable earth into ourselves so deeply, so painfully and passionately, that its essence can rise again "invisibly," inside us. We are the bees of the invisible. We wildly collect the honey of the visible, to store it in the great golden hive of the invisible.'

—Rainer Maria Rilke

'Against barbarity, poetry can resist only by confirming its attachment to human fragility like a blade of grass growing on a wall while armies march by.'

—Mahmoud Darwish

BUNTING'S HONEY

MONET IN ÁRANN

for Kathleen Loughnane

Over the sunstruck, drystone wall
we were ambushed by the sway
and scent of a July meadow—
whites of tall daisy and yarrow,
purples of scabious and cranesbill,
the bitten yellow of cat's ear,
the blue tremble of harebells,
and far more we couldn't name,

but we were caught, are caught still,
in the blurry, summery sway of it.

A QUARREL WITH THE LEXICOGRAPHERS

The dictionary is unambiguous.
It says the word comes
from '*coire*', cauldron,
but the lexicographers haven't climbed
Croaghan on Achill and looked down
from its northern flank
into silver-rimmed Loch Bunnafreva,
or trudged up Tonlegee's
brown, soggy shoulder
and seen that high sliver of light
as the mountain begins to unveil its treasure
or, as a child, scrambled up the skree skirt
of Eachla Beag, to be astounded
by a great lake hung between three peaks.

It's not just the closeness of the name
to *coeur, croí*, or *corazón* which persuades
me it's a cognate, a word-cousin,
it's the way my own heart leaps
every time I find a corrie lake, away up
in skree and heather, at the core
of a glacier-sculpted mountain.

AND AGAIN THE MOUNTAINS...

for Richard Wall

white and glittering in May sunlight,
as they fly down to Lough Inagh—
the three great buttresses of Doire an Chláir,
Binn Chorr and Binn an Choire Beag.

The mountains are indifferent
to us who love them
and don't answer to their names:
Peak by the Oak Grove Plain,
Sharp Peak,
Peak of the Small Corrie.

No medieval master builder drew up plans,
by rule of thumb, by counted cubits,
to raise this singing edifice
along the indigo lake;
no architect calculated the slants
of winter light across its tall, rough coombes

but an old ocean leaned heavily down
upon the weather-milled, river-drifted
debris of vanished mountain ranges,
pressing it to sandstone.

Aeons later, a hot, shifting earth lifted
and pinched the sandstone into a long,
crooked fold, then forged it
into a shining quartzite range
to be storm-flayed into beauty.

WICKLOW DIAMONDS

for Isabelle Vallet–Dunne

Bright as April hail, it glitters
beside the brown bog path
all the way around Loch Bray—
two lakes, and today,
two calm blue eyes, regarding heaven.

Our heads are light as cirrus clouds
our hearts bright as those
of this year's kid goats
who scramble over scree
at the lake's far edge.

After three weeks of sun
the bog path springs under our feet;

after months of fearful confinement
we are restored to friendship,
to our companionship of the hills;

four hundred million years
after it cooled in darkness
granite is frost-shattered into diamonds.

23/04/2021

FOR THE BIRDS

'You must change your life'
Rainer Maria Rilke

And how we resist it, as though all change
had designs on us, yet for the birds too,
as for insects and glaciers,
for leverets and children,
change we must:

for blackbird, whose yellow, up-flung notes
and triplets fill back yards and skies,
who has sung this April week for love or lust
all morning and again at dusk
from a neighbour's blocked-off chimney pot;

for goldfinch, whose red velvet head
bobs around the feeder
and the martins who fly far, far to dig,
with little beaks, deep homes in sand;

for feather-trousered eagle,
vice-gripper, soarer on thermals,
sky-lord who claimed and named high places
long before any Fionn or Arthur lived;

for the bird whose harsh unwelcome rasp
annoyed us out of sleep on childhood mornings
when we longed to hear instead,
summer's two cool, perfect notes—cuck-oo, cuck-oo.

Who, then, could ever have believed
that poor, tuneless corncrake
and her down-black chicks
would vanish from the tough, long grass

or that pigeon flocks so vast they darkened
America's skies, hunted for sport and pigeon pies,
would be reduced to one poor bird,
who died, imprisoned, in a Cincinnati zoo.

Or who could believe
that little garden birds whose forebears
brought song from Australia
so many million years ago,

who, when the world fell silent, sang on,
who gave us heart this long, last year,
are being starved and poisoned
by our careless ways.

We know it's not too late, but almost,
the cost already runs too high—
we, who still have a choice,
must change our lives.

09/06/2021

DIE-BACK

for Sabine Springer

Young, spear-leaved birches
have magicked the motorway
into a shimmering, green corridor
and everything is light-drunk May.

Along the narrower roads,
regal beech condescend
to sycamore between
forsaken farmhouses
and fleeing bungalows
as hawthorn shakes out
its white blossom
to frill the small fields.

Some plants, some creatures,
die quietly in corners,
are gone before they are noticed.
A species, even, can disappear discreetly,
with no official count-down,
without the drama
of an asteroid or an ice-age.

It's hard, though,
for an ash tree to hide—
like sycamores,
ashes are sociable and flighty

Yet, as we drive west,
all across this greening country
they are surrendering—
they are coming out
of the hedgerows
with their thin hands up.

II

DÚCHAS

'Sweet Tyrone among the bushes'
The Rock, Sixmilecross, Loughmacrory,
she spoke the names affectionately,
all the consonants softened,
all the vowels lengthened—
Pomeroy, Beragh, Omagh —
hamlets, villages, towns
that had surrounded her childhood—

To us children,
summer-holiday names
almost as exotic as Samarkand
but we sometimes wondered
which rock among so many?
Six miles from where?
Who was MacRory
and how did he get his own lake?
And, later, what king and why an apple?

But later still, those names shrilled—
night raids, armed soldiers shouting
in the kitchen of our small, favourite aunt,
bewildered young cousins interned,
armoured cars and murderous
night-time road-blocks
and then, a bombing, heinous, catastrophic.

What's in a place-name—
a hill where a glacier paused, exhausted;
a rise or hollow
where the earth's crust crumpled,
a stony, embattled river-crossing?

Is it power, dramatic incident
or primal poetry,
that allows specific syllables
first stick to field,
forest, house or hill?
—before life and time
play on them
to ring joybells
or knells of dread
inside our heads.

And can place-names
once, maybe, tenderly spoken—
Wounded Knee, Xwéda, Babi Yar, Hiroshima,
Kosovo, Kabul, Bucha, Omagh—
ever be cleansed of their pain?

And what's in any name?

What does *omphalos* mean?
Or *dúchas*?
What does *dúchas* mean
and why has such violence
been wreaked in its gentle name?

'I have a great desire that you should endeavour to keep the instrument as well as the music alive, and you are perhaps the only person who can now do it...'

Dr. James MacDonnell to Edward Bunting,
28 September 1840

Three years ago the walls
of the Bastille were breached
and today the Irish Volunteers,
Protestant and Papist,
march down a Belfast Street,
fire three *feux de joie*,
then enter the Linen Hall
to forge a new state
through keen debate.

Nearby, in the Exchange Rooms,
an old order seems to breathe its last—
eleven harpers, six blind,
have taken their several paths
to Doctor MacDonnell's festival of harps.

The eldest is blind Denis Hempson,
last player in the old style,
who plucks brass strings with crooked nails,

then blind, dapper Arthur O'Neill,
who has given away his spare good suit
to harper Pat McAlinden of Oriel,
who went rambling and won't arrive;

here is blind Rose Mooney whose feckless maid
once pawned her mistress's harp
and best petticoat for drink;
and there is harper Williams from Wales,
fated to die, too soon, on the grey-green waves

and, listen, here is young William Carr
who plays 'The Dawn of Day'.

The other six, come-down gentlemen some,
are dressed in grey or drab-coloured cloth.
Their old patrons are generations gone
to France, to Spain, to the tuneless grave,

but the old music still travels
Ireland's metalled
and unmetalled roads
played to all,
regardless of creed or name,
who esteem music and song,
and keep a house good enough
to afford bed, board and maybe drink
to a harper for a week or a month.

A good hostess might, with luck,
be repaid with a tune in her name,
fine enough to catch the ear
and be held in trust
by some country piper or fiddler

or even by the very young man—
a musical prodigy it is agreed,
an opinionated youth, a few claim—
who now moves among the harpers,

steady as a bee-keeper,
jotting down air after air,
noting shakes and graces,
double slurs and turns, delighting
in the most ancient tunes,
seeking out the nimble felicities
of the harper's art.

Gentry of the first fashion,
from Belfast and its environs
pay half a guinea to listen
and look on with attention
and Theobald Wolfe Tone looks in
but his mind is on revolution.

Decades before young Edward Bunting dies
a great French empire will rise and fall;
Wolfe Tone's revolution will have failed
yet Bunting's life will still be held in thrall
by this treasure he garners in the Exchange hall.

But now the harpers, mostly old, display
to each other and salvage
airs which remember and relay
griefs, gaieties and passions
of spirits long parted from their clay;

for what do a musician's hands ever hold
but the hammered treasure of the human soul?

PASCAL

The eternal silence of these infinite spaces terrifies me.
—Blaise Pascal

You understood so much as you stood in awe
of our long-armed swirl of stars
burning their huge hearts out—
yet you didn't know that there were other,
far more distant, worlds of light,
that our spinning, sea-blue earth,
our sun and sister planets,
are smaller than salt grains
in the dark, rushing theatre of space.
You didn't know that we,
our eyebrows, livers, ankles, thumbs,
are forged of old stars blown to dust
then, somehow, sprung to life,
that our distant, minute, unthinking ancestors
might have bubbled up through an ocean floor
or hurtled in on the frozen fragment of a star.

You, who believed that the supreme function
of reason is to show us
that some things are beyond reason,
did you, in your faith and wondering,
still strive to fix and hold steady a platform,
high above us and our sun, to accommodate,
in golden rows, the mystery of cherubim,
seraphim, the righteous dead,
God's saints, the trinity enthroned?

We, who grew up with reason enthroned,
who have learned how to weigh a star
and measure a billion years of light,
who have blurred the plush black
of your silver-studded night
with our small, insistent lamps,

we wonder, still, what lies
beyond the rim of a universe
which may have no edge at all
in either space or time, which may fold
back upon itself in deepest mystery

as, above and around us,
planets spin out their very long
or their very short days, as red giants,
white dwarves and supernovae grow,
implode, burn out, collide
yet continue to come to birth.

SAINT-ROMAIN-DES-ÎSLES

for Chantal Vallet

Another long stroke—
a heron with yellow leather feet,
rasps off from the island reeds,

The broad green river,
flowing high road of our forebears,
runs low and calm today—
how could it ever have risen,
a torrent that flooded
the old, square house
and its barns
with clay from the Saône?

The garden wall is built of roof tiles
stood on edge. Seven tile factories
once flourished in the village—
fired clay from the Saône.

The sons of Charlemagne
met here to divide his kingdom.
Now, at the end of the long bridge,
a cloud of midges
rises and falls.

The midges are so minute
and quick, I can't see their wings
yet each one of them too
has a heart and eyes—
flying clay from the Saône.

No one remembers those
who trudged here or travelled
on horseback or by boat,
from Lyon or Rome
to raise a small church
at this river crossing and name it
for Romain, martyr of Antioch.

Outside it, other dead are remembered,
'Nos jeunes, morts pour la France à Verdun'—
dead, with a hundred thousand others
in a forest by the Meuse—

village boys who startled the waterbirds
when they swam and shouted
and raced each other out to the river island,

each beautiful young man,
once beloved of someone—
clay from the Saône,

and, like priests, princes and midges,
life jetted from a star.

THE GLANCE

In the side-chapel of the Frari
a teenage girl glances
just slightly sideways
from her gold-roofed alcove,
balancing a little child
just old enough to stand
on her blue-draped thigh.

Miraculous how Bellini
with his new-fangled oil paints
and the finest of miniver brushes
has translated this glance
with its hint of trepidation
across half a millennium.

How can the truth and tenderness,
the absolute ringing beauty
of this painting, almost transcend
the contradictions of this loveliest of cities
built on water and silt,
built on a hundred oak forests,
built on ten thousand galleys,
built on prayers and plunder,
built on trade, knowledge and art,
built on silk and gold,
built on the shoulders of slaves?

Could it be because,
with her grave, girlish face,
she might be any teenage mother,
black, brown, yellow or white,
today, or in five more centuries,
who supports a little child,
just old enough to stand,
turning him out to a future world,
far beyond the reach of her knowing
far beyond the reach, even, of her love?

THE SKY-WRAPPER OF TORCELLO

for Eiléan Ní Chuilleanáin

What a job for a young man to land—
a young angel, I mean, no cherub,
but a young fellow who might be about seventeen
if angels lived in time,
which they didn't, not even then,
at the turn of the first millennium
when a vast and dazzling mosaic
of The End of Days
was commissioned for the exit wall
of the Basilica di Santa Maria Assunta
to remind the home-going devout
and not-so-devout of Torcello,
mother island of Venice,
of death, resurrection and mercy,
of the tailored torments of hell—
a customised pit for each of the seven deadly sins—
but also of the rewards of the blessed
on the day of the Last Judgement,
believed then to be very near.

And what a handsome young angel—
athletic, nonchalant,
one of his blue-tipped wings askew
with the effort of his huge task,
his heavy golden hair matching his halo,
his tunic of gold,
his white mantle,
feather-light sandals.

His beautiful, Byzantine eyes
are focused on his work.

He is rolling up the starry firmament,
with all its fixed stars and wandering stars,
its hero stars and storied constellations.

Now that heaven and earth are no more,
there can be no further need of it.

A TECHNOLOGY

'Who will survive to shoot messages
from age to age, like swallows
joining different countries.'
　　　　　　—James Harpur, Magna Karistia

The poet writes of Brother John Clyne, the annalist,
who, in Kilkenny, one day during the great plague of 1349
'left blank parchment to continue the work
if, perchance, any man survive.'

Plague raged on, until it wore itself out
but humanity, parchment,
and Brother John's annals survived.

How late in our human story we learned the skill,
so very long after we had learned to halt
fleet herds of horses in pigment on a cave wall,
to breathe human spirit through the hollow
in a swan's wing bone,
to release a mammoth
from seeping stone.

So many more millennia
before we learned to interpret
symbols traced by a finger in dust,
scratches on ox shoulder blades,
ordered triangles pressed into clay,
inked hieroglyphs on dried papyrus,
runes carved into weather-polished rock,
letters scraped with pared goose feathers
on cured calf-skin.

II

Hand-muscles were hard-schooled
to form a perfect majuscule,

before the leap

from the furled scrolls of Alexandria
to the monk's many-leaved book,
from Gutenberg's great press
to the compositor's hot lead,
to the clacking typing pool,

and from there
to microchip, lap-top, tablet,
glimmering smart-phone screen,
until our globe is swathed
in a tissue of whirring symbols—

but a millennium from now
will anyone, perchance, survive
to interpret our cacophony,

to continue the work?

'GIRLS TRAINED IN BEAUTIFUL WRITING'

For Christopher Kelly

Like a fifth century Maria Montessori,
Saint Jerome sent sage counsel to Laeta in Rome
to give her infant daughter, Paula,
'Letters of boxwood or ivory to play with…
let her play with them, making a road to learning'.
He urged Laeta 'to guide her hand on a wax tablet…
offer her prizes for spelling'.

So it is surprising
that it was Jerome,
himself scathing of scribes who,
through ignorance or arrogance,
amended sacred texts,

odd that it should have been Jerome
who almost expunged from history
the skilled girl calligraphers
of third century Caesarea,
neglecting to mention them,

while he credited the rest of the crack team
of the great scholar, Origen of Alexandria,
the seven or more shorthand writers
who took dictation in relays,

then passed it on to the same number
of copyists to decipher it,
before the girl scribes
got to work on the famed Hexapla,

the six-columned Old Testament—
two versions in Hebrew
and four in Greek.

Oh, who were those shining girls,
those young slaves or free women,
who bent to the Hexapla?

—those third century scribes
of whom we know barely a jot.

PLANTING ROSES IN BAICHENG

The six small, old women wore working clothes,
gloves, trousers, check shirts, army fatigues,
patterned scarves over baseball visors,
and one wore a white, polka-dot, cotton bonnet.

They were planting a bed of roses
under birches in Baicheng City,
as a youngish man handed down
small rose bushes from a pick-up truck.

One thin, bow-legged, old woman
turned a curious, weathered face
towards me and straightened up
and I wanted to ask her,

a witness from inside history,
about her girlhood,
about her city or village
and its happenings.

For a full minute,
we were stilled
in each other's gaze.
What did she wonder?

I come from a village
on the other side of the earth.
What happened there?
And what did I know of it then,

what do I know now?
What could I tell her?
It looks good to be out planting roses
on a sunny street in old age

but what do I know,
what do I really know?

HEAVEN LAKE, JILIN PROVINCE

To right and left rise steep,
skree-rough, basalt slopes;
below us, sickle-wings swoop
across a cauldron of cloud;
through grey, sheeps' wool fog
a few peaks appear.

Then the wind whips
at our raincoats
and furls the clouds up
over the ankles
of a round rim of peaks
as the great caldera lake appears.

The lake now shimmers,
huge and blue,
mirrors a sky which clears fast,
as the crowd sighs and jostles
closer to a roped cliff edge
where a hundred smartphones are held aloft.

In the earth's long memory
this is a very young lake,
recently born of fire and rending;

in short human memory.
it is a very old lake, a mirror dropped
by a careless young sky princess.

Dong Zhu, the woman
who wrote of how the ripping
of the earth's crust which,
while it raised mountain ranges,
also transported the habitat of a flower,
gently taps my arm and points up

to where geology and myth both sing true.
A scarf of fine, white cloud
is flung into the heavens
and, above the round, bright lake,
the wind dances with it,
faster, higher, wilder, faster.

DELETE CONTACT CARD

It's happening more often now—
going through my contacts list
I find the name of an old friend,
a decade or more older than me,
with whom I spent sunlit afternoons,

laughing and talking about life and poetry
and I don't delete the card—
as though a computer list could
hold a soul for a month, a year, or more
in some limbo or bardo.

Rain falls on the red bushes;
the talkative postman
still delivers books and letters,
and, with a small thump,
a goldfinch lands on the window feeder.

Life does go on without the dead
and, no matter how much we wish it,
we won't ever know for certain
whether or not the dead watch over us
until our own cards await deletion.

What we do know now, better
than we used to, is the worth
of that honeycomb of hours
spent laughing and talking—
the sunwashed, unwasted hours
of human contact.

III

NEEDLEWORK

For Róise Goan

Needlework,
the festival of broken needles
at the start of Japan's new year
when kimono makers gathered
to pray for improved skills
to give thanks
to their diminutive, broken tools,
to tenderly deposit old needles
broken in silk.

Needlework,
how long, how far back,
do the tough threads run—

bone, horn, mammoth ivory needles,
or awls that pierced and laced with sinew
furs and hides that allowed
our foremothers, forefathers to walk
northwards, to stitch tents
in snowy edgelands;

wooden, iron needles that wrought nets
to trap lusting, homing salmon.

Needlework,
which granted poor women
a small sway over destiny—
the knitter, lacemaker,
embroiderer or seamstress,
who, under a candle or an oil lamp,

over an open fire, clothed children
dreaming in the next room,
stitched them an apprenticeship,
a dowry, an education,
a sea-passage to a new land;

the two proud old sisters in east Tyrone,
half-blind from the white linen embroidery
that had made their brother a priest;

the woman from Ranafast
who rested two needles
and the in-curled sleeve
of an Aran cardigan on the table,
pointed to the ceiling
and said, 'I knit the roof'.

THE ORANGE RUCKSACK

'They change their sky, not their soul, who rush across the sea.'
                                                              —Horace

For Jessie Lendennie

That welcome 'thump, thump,'—
—a procession of suitcases, plastic-swathed,
red-ribbon marked, world-weary,
designer-shiny, poverty-stricken, begins

to move in solemn half-circuits or almost-circuits,
before each bag is grasped and hauled
off overlapping rubber mats
back into one human life.

I never trust that mine will arrive, not since
that first flight when I was sixteen and waited
at Orly airport for an orange rucksack,
bought in an army surplus shop in Liffey Street.

With its new-nylon stiffness and smell,
it whispered Versailles, art, romance
the wing-wide world, and a transfigured me.
I stuffed it full of anxieties and mended jeans.

When, at last, it nudged past
the hawk-watched plastic flaps
one of its orange ties had opened
and it had begun to spill out its innards.

It looked brasher, cheaper, than the other luggage.
I caught it as it tried to trundle past, trussed it up,
hefted it onto my back and, terrified and happy,
stepped out into the hot, Parisian afternoon.

AND WHERE WERE YOU BROUGHT UP?

—an old-fashioned question—
I was brought up
within sight of a mountain,
within hearing of the sea,
on the edge of a village,
in the tension between my parents,
two good people who saw the world differently
and since neither ever succeeded
in bending the other to his or her will,
in their fifty years together there were silences
long and taut as a piano wire.

They loved their work,
and the six of us,
although they rarely said so,
so they must have loved each other too,
though they'd, long ago,
lost courage to voice it.

THE HIGHEST HOUSE

His mother came, he said,
from half-way up a valley in Fanad.
Theirs was the last house in the valley,
she'd said, where the children weren't hired out
to a farmer in Tyrone or the Lagan.

Once, further west, I drove three miles
up a bog road, in the dark, to a house so high
it was named for the crag-roosting king of birds—
a small, lit-up hostel under the hilltop, it rocked
with young life—hikers, holiday-makers,
from Japan, Germany, Holland.

The cottage had been bought, extended,
after the death of an old, cranky man,
who was hired at the fair,
for six months at the age of six,
instead of at the usual nine or ten.
The boy's sister, said the hostel owner,
was hired out at the age of seven,
"No one," he said, shaking his head,
"was that poor".

What did he, what do we, know now
of the humiliations of hunger and servitude,
of having your arm-muscles felt
at a hiring-fare,
of the toss-penny chance
of landing in a good place
or a bad one,
of the slow burn
of anger
down the generations?

THE FIRST HE'D HEARD OF IT

'...the great Irish sin of respectability'
                    —John B. Keane

Sometimes it was the doctor's wife
who drove the girl at dawn
to the house of refuge and shame.

My uncle drove a hackney car,
told of driving a girl, her baby
and parents on the way *'to give*
the child a better chance in life',
the girl crying, crying in the back seat
and not wanting at all to part with her.

There were the three girls in my year
who didn't return to school the September
after doing their Intermediate Cert
and giving birth.

And there was the man from Inishowen
who sat beside me on the bus
from Galway to Letterkenny
who nipped off more than once for a drink
and who told me of a much older sister
who had worked in a shirt factory in Derry
and how fond they had been of each other
and how, when she was ill and dying,
he had run, barefoot, in the dark,
to hammer on the doctor's door

and of how, years later, in Scotland
he was in love with a girl
and they were engaged
and the priest read the riot act to him
and asked who did he think he was
to try to marry a respectable girl,
and that was the first he'd heard of it.

ALL GONE

*The immense call of the particular, despite the earthly law
that sentences memory to oblivion.*

—*Czeslaw Milosz*

A century ago, when my mother's brother
was a very small boy
and his father was heading to Dungannon
with the horse and trap,
he used always ask him to bring home
a piano and glasses.

And, somehow or other, the piano and glasses
had always fallen off on the way home
and a great search was made of the trap
up, down and under, until a penny toffee
or a poke of clove drops was found.

And my mother had a china doll
who used appear every Sunday
on a chair in the hallway
of their small cottage
until the same brother
shot it with a pellet gun.

And a century later
hardly anyone remembers this
nor do they really matter,
the trillions of family stories
which, every day, drift down
a billion rivulets
into Lethe's indifferent waters.

Against the glitter and stench
of battles won and lost,
against treaties wearily signed,
injustices righted or endured,

famines suffered,
how can a small boy's dream of urbanity,
a small girl's grief at the loss of a doll,
possibly matter?

Yet stories of dreams and grief
are what bind the world together,

like the swallows I saw nesting
between neon signs in a hot city in China—

they were just like our own.

FRIDAY

The moon shines full over Creeslough,
may it guide all the dear souls home,
they died on an ordinary Friday,
their week's work, their school work done.

Brothers, mothers, fathers and sisters
at a cash machine, a post office queue,
a birthday cake never delivered,
a young beauty, three dear children too.

Neighbours with bare hands and shovels
helped firemen to dig out their friends,
a man worked with a digger until daybreak
when the last little body was found.

A whale song can cross the Atlantic,
from Cuba to a Donegal shore,
a lament can carry far farther,
from Zimbabwe, Australia to Doe.

The Arranmore and Inishowen disasters
are remembered in Donegal still
the train that derailed in a valley, and now,
Creeslough, where the darlings were killed.

Red fuchsia still blooms around Muckish,
late blackberries hang on the briars,
but grief's flood has ripped through the village
for the dead and for those who survive.

May God guide the bereaved, the heartstricken,
those wounded in body and mind,
and the dear ones who died on a Friday,
all their life's work, their life's loving done.

NOW, AS THEN

for Maureen Murphy

'You'll be following the crows
over the hills for that yet'—
a reproach heard a dozen times
from my mother, as I,
or any of us,
threw out a scrap of food

—A vision of ragged-skirted women running,
silhouetted against a curved skyline,
and the crows, the crows,
growing ever more distant—

but I didn't wonder until recent years
where the saying came from—
from her own mother, maybe, born
at the height of the land war,

or her mother's father, who was born
the year of emancipation,
was almost a young man, was old enough
to cut and set the seed potatoes in 1845

with no inkling of what
was coming over the hills—
the silent, murdering fungus,
and then, the clamorous crows.

And, battling the silence, what now,
besides an odd adage, is passed down
those three long generations
from *aimsir an drochshaol?*

—thrift, caution, maybe distrust of the earth—
that phrase my friend inherited, 'A foot
of counter is better than an acre of land.'
but maybe, too, the knowledge

that now, as then,
a famine is caused,
not by wantonness or indolence
but by inequity and indifference,

and, now, as then,
something can be done,
and, now, as then,
history will be our judge.

IV

A SONG AT IMBOLC

*'Now at spring's wakening, short days are lengthening
and after St. Bridget's Day, I'll raise my sail.'*
                                    —*Antoine Ó Raifteirí*

A blind man, on a stone bridge in Galway
or the road to Loughrea, felt the sun's rays
in his bones again and praised the sycamore and oak,
crops still drowsy in the seed, wheat, flax and oats.
His song rising, he praised Achill's eagle, Erne's hawk
and in beloved Mayo, young lambs, kids, foals,
and little babies turning towards birth.

Blind Raftery invoked Bridget, Ceres of the North,
born into slavery at Faughert, near Dundalk
to an Irish chieftain and a foreign slave.
Why, of all small girls in so distant a century born
is she honoured, still, in place-names, constant wells,
new rushes plaited to protect hearth, home and herd?

Bridget, goddess, druidess of oak, or saint—a girl
who gifted her father's sword to a beggar for bread,
we, who have wounded the engendering seas and earth,
beg you to teach us again, before it grows too late,
your neglected, painstaking arts of nurture and of care.

TAKING THE BRUNT OF IT

I pick them up in the sunny park every morning,
to bring home and put in a glass jug.
They are mostly short-stemmed,
bent and broken by April gusts.
I did not know there were so many different kinds—
orange-fringed suns, yellow trumpets,
dainty white dancers, saffron flouncers.

The brave narcissi, up
and out on strong green stems,
taking the brunt of spring storms,
lifting their heads to the sun—
a few young ones snap at the root
but, mostly, it's the older ones,
with weakened stems,
which bend and break.

And in this storm
which rips across the world,
which has grounded air fleets,
and emptied teeming streets,
it's the older ones,
who sit, heads nodding,
in tall-backed chairs,
who try to smile into the phone,
so many different beloved ones,
who take the brunt of it.

LIGHT IS WHAT DAYS ARE MADE OF—

it pulls the daffodil up out of dark earth,
prompts the eagle and the stub-tailed wren to nest
and draws the humpback whale north with its song.

Stones, warm on the morning sea-shore, know it.
Our sun is so much older than them—
such tempests of grief it has scanned
yet light, like love, eternally draws us on.

JANUARY DAWN

Across the low, far horizon
stride the hail showers.
Between them
pink embers rest on the sea.

PRIMAL

This luminous morning, the regular thump
of brown waves almost drowns out
the delicious tock and susurrus of surf
backrushing seawards through shingle,
sieving through pebbles of granite,
limestone, sandstone, quartz, flint—
earth's layering, burning, rending history,
reduced to a shining, salty jumble.

And someone who was here earlier—
this morning or yesterday evening,
has set up an alignment of seven
sea-smoothed fragments of red brick
which greet the rising sun across the tide.

And nothing will do me but to line up
more and more sea-rounded cliff-jetsam—
bricks from a long-gone lime-kiln—
to set up row after red sun-struck row.

BIRDS AND LOVERS

for Kerry and Sean Hardie

It cannot be true that birds
bring forth the sun
but this January dawn,
against an orange, eastern sky,
three silhouettes,
swans, beat southwards
low over the horizon;
soon, a raucous
of herring-gulls
pulses high overhead
and a flock of plovers,
invisible among shingle,
rises in an epiphany,
then swerves back
over a foam-flittered sea-edge.

Nearby, a young man in a padded jacket
has been skipping stones
into the future while, behind him,
a young woman, blue, woollen hat pulled
down over her fair hair,
perches on a boulder.

Now, they watch the great gold coin rise,
second by second,
to cast a broad bright path
across the tide to them;

three ships, loaded shopping trolleys,
roll across the horizon;
four windows on the hill,
golden mirrors, flash their messages
and the young sun-god strides out again.

FROM THE TRAIN WE SEE NO STRAIGHT LINE

as they reach the curved beach,
the far-fetched waves fold down
on themselves at a first taste of sand;

northerly and southerly tides
have scalloped the heaped shingle as neatly
as the thumb-scalloped rim of an apple tart;

a sickle-winged kestrel is pinned
against the hill; a swimmer's arm
curves into and out of a pocked tide;

the shore rocks are earth-twisted, time twisted;
the shore pebbles sea-milled to ovals
and the horizon, which splits pale grey sea

from pale grey sky, which almost fools us
with its spirit-level straightness,
is a tiny segment of the world's greatest hoop.

THIS MORNING

for Jean Tuomey

This morning by the sun-bashed sea,
in which I have swum for ten minutes,
I feel younger than when I was young
in spite of my sixty-six circuits of the sun.

I have done nothing to earn joy
or health, yet today, am flooded with both.
I want to bottle this morning in a song
so that, some hail-smitten, hope-poor

winter's day, it can be poured out—
sun on salted pebbles and on me,
a flutter-swoop of sand-martins
and the whispers of a June sea.

SURREAL SHORE

Above us,
from the brand-new
cliff-edge
of a sand-dune sliced
in two, then scoured
by last week's
hard storms and high seas,
droops a curl of earth-carpet—
half a yard of stiff,
browning grassland.

Through it, long roots
of marram grass,
released from their drudgery
of anchoring sand,
waft and sway
high above our heads—
float, free, free as seagrass.

SOUP

A plastic container
of frozen vegetable soup
has been warming in the sink
since this morning.

When I slip the block
into a saucepan
it breaks up
and melts quickly

Lately, when I see this
I think of a shelf of ice
bigger than greater Paris

which has broken
off Antarctica
to float in the Weddell Sea
and I wonder
if all the king's horses

and all the king's men
and all our technologies
and all of us
will ever be able

to put Antarctica
together again.

THE NEWS FROM TRAMORE

At the near end of this dune-hidden, northern beach,
there used to be two enormous grey globes—
fisherman's floats—until sand,
like a boa-constrictor, swallowed them whole
or someone's small tractor hauled them home.

Our beach-booty was a Caribbean sea-bean,
a giant whelk shell, a mermaid's ripped purse,
or a green glass float—
a fortune-teller's unintelligible globe.

Half a century later, how lovely it looks,
the mile-long, empty, blonde beach
until we notice that the shingle
is deep-rimmed
in sea-battered drink-cans,
in eroded, broken plastic,
in single, sea-flittered trainers.

How beautiful it looks—that tangle of blue,
green and purple ropes and nets
until we notice the choked, starved gannet.

How mysterious that big object,
low down on the sunny winter shore,
until we draw near and find,
staring at us, an old, chunky television,
its name branded in a foreign script.

What urgent news is it trying to relay?
Why can we not understand
what it struggles to say?

FOUR WONDERFUL SOUNDS

This evening, four wonderful sounds—

The harsh warm marram grass on sand dunes
brilliant with lark song

The soft puttering of the ocean
in the rock pools

The wild alarm of plovers on the machair
at my approach

The whisper of barnacles to each other
as I laid my head down amongst them.

v

AND NOW THE BABIES

And now the babies
and their mothers
and their folded buggies
hurry west in trains
and fathers, husbands, brothers
must all become heroes again
and on both sides,
the dark green munitions
pile high again
and, again, old Mother Courage
rattles her old, bloodied cart
and although, long ago,
we held hands and sang
no one can remember again
no one can figure out again,
how to give peace a chance.

31/05/23

THE SLAUGHTER OF THE INNOCENTS

We weren't shielded,
so young we learned about it,
about what happened in that far country,
about the shepherds and angels and wise men,
we rhymed it off in a classroom with an open fire
and long wooden forms that rocked.

Yet, even at four or five
it was a puzzle why God
who was good and could do anything
let the bad king kill all the little boy babies
while his own baby escaped
and no one stopped the cruel soldiers.

This midwinter
in that far country
there are no shepherds,
no angels, no wise men,
the sky is bright
but not with stars

Yesterday, a friend told me
of three young brothers,
all doctors, who worked
day and night, for months,
in broken hospitals
and who, last week,
were all killed within two days.

One slaughter of innocents
has begotten another
slaughter of innocents;

babies die in smoking rubble
and neither God,
nor our evolved consciousness,
nor man nor woman
stops the cruel soldiers.

24/12/23

THROUGH IRON RAILINGS

We have arrived too late to enter;
between us and the ruined spans
of the wide-arched abbey
a hawthorn bush is in bloom.

A sparrow alights, takes flight,
the branch bounces back—
scatters May's rough perfume.

TURLOUGH HILL

for Margaret Duffy and Pascal Bradley

Some places resist interrogation
but still are rich in giving—
places like this one,
that draws us
to leave our everydays,
to trudge up a cattle-trodden,
tractor-rutted lane,
to climb up through blossom
and sharp-edged stone
as into a song.

This huge, angled, hilltop enclosure
asks a hundred questions,
yields few answers—
did people sacrifice here,
or bring their beloved dead
for ravens to carry their earth essence
into an untroubled sky—
was this a court of law,
a place of congress for many tribes,
a place of festival at harvest time?

Because nobody wrote
nobody will ever know.

Yet, with its many entrances,
this was no fortress.

Early peoples who came here
also left a high burial mound,
foundations of a hundred huts
and scattered hazelnut shells.

Today, exhausted at the hilltop,
we are rewarded
with rapture under a high sky,
with a new sweep of vision
out past Bell Harbour
to the islands and the glittering sea,
to the stepped and light-shaken,
the flower-filled, catacombed hills,
to the valley and the far, green plains—

and the sharing of all of this
with those we know
and those we don't,
with the companion beside us,
with those who built this great enclosure
and those still centuries from birth,
is like the sharing of a dance or a song
like the sharing of any beauty, any pain,
a soul-marking, an enduring bond.

INVENTORY AT ST CRONAN'S WELL

One string of Buddhist worry beads,
One blue pottery nativity scene,
One triad of Hindu gods
wearing two blue miraculous medals,
One tiny brass bell on an orange ribbon,
One silver whistle on an orange loop,
One red velvet headband,
One red crocheted heart with a pearl,
One large limpet shell,
One child's eraser,
One baby's soother,
Two gents' striped handkerchiefs,
Assorted ribbons, hair-ties, bracelets,
An underwater glitter of coins

And beside the clean, u-shaped,
stone well, in sunshine,
Hips on a wild rose bush,
Haws on a hawthorn,
Sloes on a blackthorn,
Winged seeds on a sycamore,
A stonechat's and a blackbird's song
entangled in the brambles,
A stone cairn nearby
And a white cup with a blue rim
hung head-high on an ash branch.

Was thirst ever so candid,
Was hope ever so manifest,
Was a source ever so honoured,
Were banners ever lifted so high,
In life's bright battle with illness,
Love's long debate with oblivion?

EIGHT MARYS, FOUR BRIDGETS, THREE KATES

Four hundred left Achill that morning.
Thirty-two would come home on the train.
Torn shawls on the quay stones of Westport,
some never saw Achill again.

In Scotland to earn the back-rent,
tattie-hokers the name they would know,
here they were Mary and Bridget,
Pat, Sibby, Kate, Honor and Joe.

At Cloughmore on June the fourteenth,
four hookers lay out from the quay,
the currachs were rowed out to meet them
and the *Victory* headed away.

The steamer was sighted near Westport,
girls crowded all on to one side,
all singing and laughing and waving.
The wind changed, the boat gybed and capsized.

Young Tom Burke and Edward O'Malley
saw it happen and rowed to their aid;
on the quayside in Westport they laid them,
eight Marys, four Bridgets, three Kates.

Two days later the iron track was opened,
on the first train those coffins came home,
the boreens were black nearing Achill,
with poor people who'd walked there to mourn.

An old man was drowned and a small girl,
Mary Doogan, the blind fiddler's wife,
from The Valley the three Malley sisters,
each one in the flower of young life.

In Blenaskill the Cooneys keened Nancy
and Joseph and young Martin too,
such a blight had never struck Achill,
such a sorrow Currane never knew.

They sleep by the sea in Kildavnet
where white lilies grow tall near the brine,
and maybe the gentle St Davnet,
helped those mothers and fathers survive.

It was poverty forced them to leave home
and greed causes poverty still,
poor people still put out in small boats
and young bodies wash in with the tide.

OUGHTMAMA

In memory of Tim and Mairéad Robinson

'The Bosom of the Gap'
Who so aptly named this valley?
Something about it sings
'Be at ease and rejoice'.

Scabious, purple knapweed and yarrow
sway high above August grass
while eye-bright, self-heal and black medic
assure us that illness may pass.

The holy well's drystone enclosure
shelters fuchsia, wild strawberries, and ferns.
A source welcomes the hopeful and heartsore
even in our anxious times.

How sheltered the dip in limestone
where three churches nestle, in ruins.
On a stone font two animals tussle
necks entwined for a millennium.

I have come here so often in trouble,
descended the steps to the well,
glimpsed the cuckoo fly down the valley,
seen three fox cubs at play on the hill.

Something about Ouchtmama
makes me want to lie quietly down
in its tangles of flowers and grasses,
forget sorrow, and then carry on.

SINGER

i.m. Ruby De Búrca Connolly, 2003–2022

I knew you only as a little, brown-haired girl
and now, a young woman,

you are gone
leaving a crater, a caldera, an inland sea
of grief where you used to be.
You are gone as if you had been on loan
to the green planet which you so loved.

Yesterday, in the house of that good friend,
just hours after doctors removed tubes
which supported the last sparks of your life,
we met your stunned young mother
your heart-stricken father,
your grandmother,
all in a daze of sorrow,
a labyrinth of sorrow.

And, today, in a deep valley
where, even in May sunshine, beech buds
were small, furled, brown umbrellas,
and bluebells bowed their blue heads
and a river ran brightly over granite rocks
I thought all day of you, little singer,
gone out of the world and of how, yesterday,

as we left and closed the gate
of that good friend's house
and stepped off the path,

there, on the road, was the body
of a young thrush, the tree-top singer,
brown wing-feathers fanned wide,

and the singing heart stopped.

AMOR

So, as we know there was a beginning
and an evolution to our blue globe
our one flaming star, our swinging galaxy,
our star-shaped bodies,
our convoluted intelligence,
so, too, there must have been
a beginning, an evolution, to love,
a moment, even,
when love emerged on our planet.

We know that the sheep licks
and loves a mottled new-born lamb,
that the vixen loves her cub,
the cow, the elephant, her calf,
so did that terrible entrance,
the pain of live birth,
make small lives precious,
giving birth, too, to love?

But, if so, what of the bustling duck
who leads a line of downy noise?
What of the blue-tit or eagle
whose wings labour all springtime long
in service to their clamouring young?
This looks very much like love
so is love engendered by warm blood?

Yet the cobra builds a nest on the forest floor
and coils around her clutch;
the crocodile buries her nest
of foliage and twigs

in river mud, then,
like Moses's sister,
stands, vigilant, nearby.
Later, her ferocious mate
will tenderly carry their babies
in his jagged jaws.

And what of the ocean's depths—
all that swims, scuttles, drifts
down in the dark or the half-dark—
does some germ of tenderness
abide there too
among all the tentacled,
the red-toothed hunters,
among the long-lived sharks?

OLD FRIEND

Today, light-shot, blue-silver, bridal-lace-trimmed,
as it kisses the shingle,
yesterday, leaden grey-green but still bridal-lace-trimmed
as it hammered the sand.

The sea—sky-mirror, mood-mirror—
after last night's storm the foam clumped
on the tideline is raw, shivering meringue,
which tears off in the wind
and scuds along the shore in tufts.

Long ago, on a breezy island in summer
I saw a group of laughing young men on a beach,
as one threw great clumps of gathered foam
up into the wind.

And soon, we too, after so many storms,
so many waves crested and so many tumbled
into thin, then thicker, creamy then
white, whiter, whitest foam,

we will be foam on the wind ourselves
nothing left of us in this world
but what we have remembered to give away—

    the sea, the sea,
    sky-mirror, mood-mirror, old friend.

NOTES AND ACKNOWLEDGMENTS

p.16: *Coire (Gaelic)*: Cauldron, Deep mountain hollow.
p.25: *Dúchas (Gaelic)*: What is native, natural, heritage.
p.60: *Aimsir an drochshaol (Gaelic)*: Lit. 'The bad times', i.e. The Great Famine 1845–48.

'A Song at Imbolc': Commissioned by Galway 2020, European Capital of Culture.

'Light is What Days are Made of': commissioned by Radió Telefís Éireann as part of its *Shine Your Light* project Easter Poetry Ireland, 2021.

'Bunting's Honey': commissioned by *Cruit Eireann*/Harp Ireland and set to music by harpist, Aisling Lyons, to mark the 250th anniversary of the birth of musician and music collector, Edward Bunting.

'Then, as Now': commissioned for film, *Bealach an Fhéir Ghortaigh*/ Hunger's Way, directed and produced by Vincent Woods and Edwina Guckian for Strokestown International Poetry Festival, 2021.

'For the Birds': commissioned by Department of Zoology, UCD, in partnership with Poetry Ireland, for Of *Claws and Hooves* and Meadows, published by, Poetry Ireland, 2023.

Fronticepiece: Rilke quote from A*head of All Parting: Selected Poetry and Prose of Rainer Maria Rilke*, translated by Stephen Mitchell and published by Modern Library, 1995.

p.30: Pascal quote is from his *Pensées* (1670, ed. L. Brunschvicg, 1909)

p.65: Antoine Ó Raifteirí translation, author's own.

Acknowledgments are due to the following publications and broadcasts in which some of the poems first appeared: *Five Points, Archipelago, Poetry Ireland Review, Cyphers, Irish Pages, The Irish Times, New Hibernia Review, RISE (Review of Irish Studies in Europe), C`oillte Dúchasacha Chontae Dhún na nGall, Den Kreis Gezogen auf Dem Echo Der Wellen, Carnets du ShannOdet,* The Poetry Programme RTE1, Sunday Miscellany, Arena, Poetry File, Lyric FM, The Shaking Bog Podcast.

Sincere thanks are due to Áosdána, The Arts Council of Ireland and Dún Laoghaire-Rathdown County Council for their invaluable financial support during the writing of this collection, to the Heinrich Böll Cottage, Achill, and the Centre Culturel Irlandais, Paris, for their warm hospitality, and also to Poetry Ireland for their ongoing support.